RED CLOUD

BY MARIA NELSON

Gareth Stevens
PUBLISHING

Please visit our website, www.garethstevens.com. For a free color catalog of all our high-quality books, call toll free 1-800-542-2595 or fax 1-877-542-2596.

Library of Congress Cataloging-in-Publication Data

Nelson, Maria.
  Red Cloud / Maria Nelson.
     pages cm. — (Native American heroes)
  Includes bibliographical references and index.
  ISBN 978-1-4824-2692-2 (pbk.)
  ISBN 978-1-4824-2693-9 (6 pack)
  ISBN 978-1-4824-2694-6 (library binding)
  1. Red Cloud, 1822-1909—Juvenile literature. 2. Oglala Indians—Kings and rulers—
Biography—Juvenile literature. 3. Red Cloud's War, 1866-1867—Juvenile literature. 4.
Bozeman Trail—History—Juvenile literature. I. Title.
  E99.O3N45 2015
  978.0049752440092—dc23
  [B]

                                         2014049287

Published in 2016 by
Gareth Stevens Publishing
111 East 14th Street, Suite 349
New York, NY 10003

Copyright © 2016 Gareth Stevens Publishing

Designer: Laura Bowen
Editor: Kristen Rajczak

Photo credits: Cover, p. 1 F. A. Rinehart/Hulton Archive/Getty Images; cover,
pp. 1–24 (series art) Binkski/Shutterstock.com; p. 5 Department of the Interior/
Wikimedia Commons; p. 7 Science & Society Picture Library/SSPL/Getty Images;
p. 9 MPI/Stringer/Getty Images; p. 11 Nikater/Wikimedia Commons; p. 13
DEA Picture Library/De Agostini/Getty Images; p. 15 Kean Collection/Getty Images;
p. 17 C. D. Arnold/Wikimedia Commons; p. 19 Library of Congress/
Wikimedia Commons; p. 21 Transcendental Graphics/Getty Images.

Printed in the United States of America

CPSIA compliance information: Batch #CS15GS: For further information contact Gareth Stevens, New York, New York at 1-800-542-2595.

CONTENTS

Boldface words appear in the glossary.

Hero for All

Red Cloud was a great leader of the Sioux (SOO) tribe. He was the only Native American in the West to win a war against the United States. Red Cloud's **devotion** to his people makes him a true Native American hero.

Great Beginnings

Red Cloud was born in 1822 near the Platte River in present-day Nebraska. His father died when he was young, and Red Cloud grew up with his mother's brother, Smoke. Smoke was a leader of the Oglala group of Sioux.

Sioux village

7

Red Cloud became a great hunter and fighter. As a young man, he took part in **raids** of nearby tribes, the Pawnee and Crow. Red Cloud began to be known as a leader among his people.

A US Take-Over

The Sioux and settlers heading west were peaceful until the 1860s. In 1865, gold was found in Montana. The US Army began building **forts** along the **route** to get there. The new route was called the Bozeman Trail.

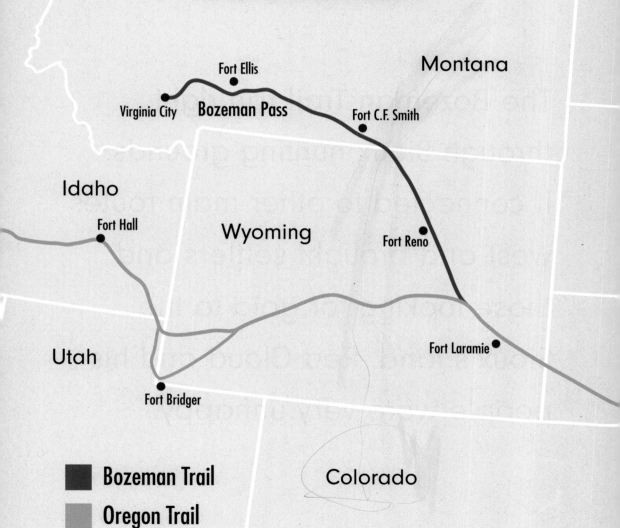

UNITED STATES

Montana

Fort Ellis

Virginia City **Bozeman Pass**

Fort C.F. Smith

Idaho

Fort Hall

Wyoming

Fort Reno

Utah

Fort Laramie

Fort Bridger

Bozeman Trail

Oregon Trail

Colorado

The Bozeman Trail ran right through Sioux hunting grounds. It connected to other main routes west and brought settlers and those looking for gold to the Sioux's land. Red Cloud and his people were very unhappy.

Red Cloud's War

In the early 1860s, other groups of Sioux had been forced off their land in Minnesota. Red Cloud didn't want that to happen to his people. He led **attacks** on the forts and stopped workers and settlers from traveling on the trail.

By 1866, Red Cloud and his followers had cut off all supplies to one of the forts. A group of 80 soldiers marched to stop him. They couldn't. Red Cloud's efforts successfully closed down the Bozeman Trail for 2 years.

17

Peace

The US government agreed to desert their forts and stop trying to open the Bozeman Trail. So, Red Cloud signed a peace **treaty**. It said the Sioux could keep their lands. However, the Sioux still burned down the US forts.

19

A Voice for the Sioux

The treaty didn't last. In the 1870s, the Sioux again fought for their land, though Red Cloud didn't. He did speak out about the cause, however. Red Cloud continued to voice the needs of his people for much of his life.

TIMELINE

1822 ○ Red Cloud is born.

1865 ○ Gold is found in Montana.

1866 ○ The Sioux cut off supplies to a US Army fort.

1868 ○ The Treaty of Fort Laramie is signed.

1909 ○ Red Cloud dies.

GLOSSARY

attack: a fight

devotion: the state of being loyal

fort: a building or set of buildings made especially strong to house troops or aid travelers

raid: a sudden attack

route: a course that people travel

treaty: an agreement between groups of people

FOR MORE INFORMATION

BOOKS

Sanford, William R. *Oglala Lakota Chief Red Cloud.* Berkeley Heights, NJ: Enslow Publishers, 2013.

Sterngass, Jon. *Crazy Horse.* New York, NY: Skyhorse Publishing, Inc., 2014.

WEBSITES

Sioux Nation

www.ducksters.com/history/native_american_sioux_nation.php

Read more about Red Cloud's people, the Sioux.

Tracking the Buffalo

americanhistory.si.edu/buffalo/

Native American tribes on the plains, such as the Sioux, used the buffalo for food and clothing. Learn more about it at this Smithsonian website.

INDEX